Full Moon, New Earth

Poems of Joy for the Collective Journey

Alix Moore

Rising Moon Press
Clarksburg, Maryland

Rising Moon Press
24110 Clarksburg Road
Clarksburg, MD 20871
http://www.writerswithwings.com

Book Layout © 2014 BookDesignTemplates.com
Cover by Creative Medium, Ltd.
Full Moon, New Earth/Alix Moore
ISBN 978-0692411025

To my mother, in joy

CONTENTS

Preface

I have always struggled to define my purpose here on Earth in this lifetime. I know my passion is writing, but to what end? Each time I think I know what I am here to do, time passes and things shift and I no longer feel certain that I know the purpose of this incarnation. Why do I write? What am I here to do?

This evening, in my meditation, I journeyed to the Temple of Knowledge, to see—and to seek answers from—a higher guide. I sat cross-legged in a white robe across from Father/Mother God, ate grapes, drank water, and asked them.

They said, in not quite so many words, "Remove the cover from your eyes."

And I realized that I was blindfolded and reached up, with some fear, and untied the knots, and saw. And what I saw was children, thousands upon thousands, reaching up, and out, and calling to me. "We need you! We need you!"

But something did not feel right, and I realized there was a blindfold under the blindfold I had just removed. I took this one away, and I saw adults, reaching out, praising me, wanting to learn what I knew.

But again, there was another cloth to take away. And this time I saw my family, living and gone, first family, love family, my dog. They, too, were speaking to me.

And I took off the next layer of cloth, and I saw myself, waving and asking me–for what?

And then I removed the final block, and I sat and looked at Mother/Father God, as we all sat cross-legged on the floor, and I knew.

It's so simple, my purpose.

I am here to grow.

And all these poems come from the journey of that growth. I offer them to you, for your journey, in the hope that they might be of help.

Namaste,

Alixander

Struggle

Spirit says:
*This is the true heart of healing—
to be enough. To know our own light,
to be fully present, and adequate.*

Little Sister

Little sister,
You are still so afraid.
The fear curls in your belly like a child
Eyes closed
Head buried beneath the covers.
Little sister,
Where does the fear come from?
What fear is this that curls like snakes behind your eyes,
Ready to blind you if you see or speak?
These fears
These snakes are old, old, old
The time of their power has passed
And yet, they live on—
For they mark not time in that place where they reside.
It is up to you, sister of light,
To see when the past is already past
To know when yesterday's wisdom is no longer truth,
When the closed heart is ready to open.
Oh sister!
Your fears are my fears.
Together we walk the rainbow of rebirth.
We are the light bearers,
Torch-kind,
Electric with our own daring
And the possibilities of
Our lightened selves.

Invitation

We have created this journey to invite
Spirit to settle in the house of the body.
When Spirit flies like a flag above our heads,
We stand in our challenges and do not see
That all things are ours for the asking.
When we step into a crisis,
All in our desperation,
We draw Spirit in.
For a brief time we are all parts
United.
But then life settles, and our fear
Rises like cream and separates the I from us.
Over and over we make
These troubled times
So that we may practice unity.
One day we will no longer need this dynamic.
For we will *know*,
And our yoyos will have been
Outgrown.

If You Are Sad (1)

If you are sad,
It is because you do not know
That you are powerful.
If you are angry,
That is the voice of your spirit speaking
Crying out to you: Pick up the reins of your destiny!
If you are depressed,
Maybe you have forgotten
That you are a child of god.
Happiness is there, but you must choose it
Peace is there, but you must ask for it
Joy is there, but you must feel worthy to receive it.
This, in a nutshell, is the journey of the planet:
To be worthy,
To be loved
To be one with the dance of divine.
I know you can do it.

If You Are Sad (2)

If you are sad
Your feet have forgotten that once they walked
In the Garden of Eden: that place where
We knew how magical we were,
Where we swam in love and unity.
But this bliss, unearned, was unappreciated,
And thus we left,
So that we might
Learn again of our divinity.
Ah, child!
Ah, man!
You are so magical,
So lovely.
You are incarnate bliss.
Like roses that wait for us to gather them,
So our souls bloom and bloom and one day we ourselves
Will realize
That all we have to do is reach for it,
And joy will truly be ours—
We will be one with god
And conscious of it.

A Dozen Roses

Oh, wounded child!
Will you bring roses to yourself?
Will you pick your own compassion,
Sunflower of a great soul,
And nurture it
With your heart light?
Like a scabbed wound,
The emptiness festers
Where you have poured your life
Onto everyone but you.
Empty,
You lose the will to live.
Eat!
Eat the manna of your own soul,
Small voice that says
I am worthy
Of my own life.

Shame

Shame
Is that energy that occurs
When we are told
How we are less than adequate
How we are not
Enough
And in compliance
We open the carrier bags of our bodies
And we cry out

> *Put it in! Put it in!*
> *For I have sworn*
> *To carry it.*

And many long roads later
We can no longer tell
Where the burden ends
And we begin
We, with our wings of light
All tarred and tarnished,
We, who have closed our own ears
To the song of god,
We, who have been complicit in
Our own unraveling.

That We May Know

So we are damaged
That we may know we are whole.

So we are defiled
That we may know we are pure.

So we are stoned
That we may rise again.

Except that
We are the stone.

And now
Is the same as gone.

It's still us
Trying to know that we are worthy.

Guilt

I make a boat
Of my guilt
A little sailing ship of twigs and leaves.
I set it free
In the river of time.
It carries away
All the might-have-beens and shoulds
All the ways in which fear had me stuck,
The ways in which
My ego can't let go
The times I failed myself or you.
My little ship of guilt,
May you burn
As brightly as a funeral pyre
Lighting the mermaid skies
Burning the old me free

Pictures

I release my pictures
Untrue truths
I have carried for so long.
They take wing over a new ocean
Explode in the fireworks of
My own independence day.
And here I stand
More naked and more free
Without the weight of
My own misunderstandings.

Words for the Road

You have done nothing wrong.
You are not flawed.
Your happiness is there for you to claim it
But if you can't see it, then
You yourself are not to blame.
You are complete
Without need of change
Without need of improvement.
You have been a child of god
From the moment you were born,
And all of life is just remembering.
Love yourself!
Spend time in the garden of your soul.
Remember yourself magical
Remember yourself strong
Remember yourself held in the cradle of the planet,
Rocked in the arms of gods
And all your doubts are thistledown—
One good breath, and gone.

Spirit Is

Spirit is
The only piece of us that is
Truly
Limitless.

Physical body comes
With clear delineation.
We can
Push our limits and
Ourselves,
But we remain
Grounded in the ecoscape of us.

Mental body pings and zips,
Courses like a terrier set free to hunt,
Flies over the planet in the quest for work.
Yet still, even our minds come home to rest.

Ego body is
A small noise in a vast space,
Beating the drum of feared significance.
Emotionally, we tsunami around with no boundaries,
Sharing our joy and pain like charity,
Learning to know better.

Yet Spirit, from that small huge place within,
Knows no time or space or lifetime limitations.
In Spirit we are one,

In Spirit, wise.

In Spirit we swim always in the sea of joy,

Bathed in the light of planets,

Carrying neither edges, nor regrets.

Fear Not

The first steps away from fear
Bring, predictably,
More fear to light.

> If I cease to comb the fur of my anxieties,
> What fleas will overrun my life?

> Peace is a great thing in my brain,
> But my body at midnight knows different.
> The pit roils,
> My belly is not convinced.

Fear cannot be hammered out of your way.
Instead, you might try this:
Hold a three-way conversation with
Spirit, fear, and self.
Drink decaf latte at Starbucks,
Ask

"What purpose do you hold, Fearsome?
What are you here to teach?"

You may know the answer already,
Or it may be startling to see
That the purpose of fear is not survival,
But growth,

Like a river slowed endlessly by swamp until it finds
The eternal expansion of ocean,
An explosion of brine

.

Awakening

Raven says:

You have the wings for the journey.
You have the strength. You are almost
big enough to be seen.

Fear Not, Plant Potatoes

Fear not,
Plant potatoes.
Do not give
Your money to greed
To make more money from
Suffering.
In that wealth there is
No true abundance.
Cling not
To the old ways,
For we have failed them
As surely we chose this path.
In the small heat of a potato
We hold another path:
The path of faith in dirt,
The path of faith in ourselves.
When we can hold compassion, caring, and love
In the core of our beings
We will no longer have reasons to hate ourselves.
When our inner core aligns with the integrity of god,
We will no longer know shame,
And without shame,
Fear will have no handle on our souls.
Until that time,
Play often in dirt,
And let yourself
Remember.

One More Soul

We are all still doing our work
The stuck spaces have not yet
Come clear
The lesson is patience
So hang your feet
Off the edge of your choice
In the river of running time
Let the spaces of your heart
Be open, wider than wide
Be flooded with sunshine

The lesson is patience
The time is drawing near
Just one more soul's awakening
Could turn the gears

The Ancestor Speaks

Come, my child, and sit
Come home to the hand of god
Come sit
In that place
Where all is well
And safety lives
Where the green grass feeds the lamb
And the lamb goes off to play
Or be eaten
Either outcome wonderfully okay
For there is a rightness of things
In the lap of god—
The dance of life in all its understandings.

Come, my child, and walk
Walk the path to god
That wends amid false mountains
And empty promises
Where it appears hard
And wears the face of challenges—
Illusions we can always disown.
Come, my child, and dance
The pavane of the path to god
Hand in hand in
Skirts and booted trouser legs
The dance of growth
Of polite civilizations
With deep roots—

The knowing of the land
While living above it.

Oh, child, no shame!
No shame
No guilt
No desperate sense of hurriedness.
All is not lost
We have not failed
Nothing has come to pass except to teach us.

Oh, child,
How bright the dawn day coming!
And this new earth
So far beyond our current reckoning.
Such joy!
We are almost able to imagine it.

Living Light

Death comes to those who bring light.
In the past, it came early and often,
Riding into the dawn valley through the mist,
Bearing the sword of fear,
Leaving behind another life paid to learning.
Those days are not over, but leaving.
Our souls are choosing to be light and stay living.
Yet still there is fear.
Fear of traveling lonesome,
Of change,
Of paying the price of place
For our enlightening.

You can't have it all
Is a myth
Humanity has suckled on,
A not-truth designed
To keep us dim.
But now our lights are rising:
We come awake.

Our spirits lead us through the swamps
Of our own limitations
On the path to the greatness
We have always been.
This time around we can remain,
Embodying truth,
Walking the life road with a planet

Who is herself deciding to remain,
To stay in skin
And yet be huge
Without remorse
Or hiding.

Trine

The power of the eagle
Is the power of the mother.

Old Grandmother,
You are not immune
Though your teats
Rest wrinkled by time.
Once you suckled young
And still that juice remains
Flowing beneficence
Milk of the planet
Now channeled to feed a new age.

Young Mother,
You are not exempt
Though babes clutch
And cry at your skirts.
You may offer them milk
Of the old ways
Or new milk to suckle.
Never doubt that you are
Pivotal.

Small Maid,
You are not excluded
Though your blood
Has never run its course.
Rather, you are required

To sit
At the feet of wise women teachers
And to choose your way:
To walk the old soft path
Or tread the new stars.
Choose wisely—
Much will depend upon it.

Conversations with Eagle

Eagle,
What do you ask of me?
    Breathe.
Eagle, what do you ask
Of me?
    Breathe.
    Breathe great eagle breaths.
    Let your wings lift with each
    Inspiration,
    Let your wings drop
    As you exhale.
    The power of your breath
    Is the power of wings
    Climbing up, and up, and up.
Eagle,
When do I stop?
    Never.
    Or perhaps,
    When the sun warms your wings
    And sets their tips to smoldering
    Then, perhaps, you may pause for a time,
    Floating, and breathing, and being light.

Eagle

Eagle has come now
Because she is a sunsurfer
Because she carries land
Up to the heavens
And brings the gods to earth.
Her people have shifted
And yet the shift
Is just beginning.
The need for her wisdom is clear:
The knowledge to
Breathe
Lift
Float
Rest
Poised between the new world and the old
And holding.

Jesus Speaks to the New Earth

Jesus' message was not of pain, he didn't *feel* pain.

Being entirely aligned with Light,

Light was all he could experience.

So he hung there against the earth and sky

To show us that we were also Light,

That if he could be so fully present

In his god self

As to transcend that punishment,

Then so also could we.

It was a testament to the magic of the universe.

And some of us got it, and

Prophets and seers were born.

There were those who listened, and those

Whose ears were not yet formed.

Jesus spoke,

And the sleepers heard but faintly

A distant truth.

They thought they heard this world was pain

And heaven the payment for it,

That suffering and sin defined us and set the price,

That compared to Jesus, we were lesser souls.

But those slumberous folks misheard.

And now, having lit

Two thousand candles on our collective birthday cake,

It's time to try again,

To align ourselves with the true message

From that far time of Christ:

That we are love, and love alone,
And any miracles that Jesus did
Are both our inheritance
And hope.

Listen, Sister!

Listen, Sister! They said
As they brushed my hair,
The long, long hair of my spirit self.
And as they braided flowers through my hair
The fairies came and
One by one
The lights went on.
My sisters led me to the woods
And where we walked the grass grew
The moss grew
Toadstools sprang up
Honeysuckle grew down
And as we walked we drank of it.
And I remembered
That the world is a wonderful, magical place.
That all we need to do is choose
Hold hands with those of our tribe
And walk out in it,
Into this joyful, ineffable experience
Called life.

Awake

My incandescent self
Knew god
Knew nothing of god
Believed in my own worth
Wept salt tears of shame
Struggled
Grew
Blew out the pilot light
A thousand times
(Trick candle
That never goes out!)
And here I am come
To the summit of my life
Descending from here
To the heights of my own soul
God herself wept
At my awakening

Trust

Grandmother Eagle says:

Stand in the dirt with your feet bare, the wind in your hair, and your eyes open. Walk where your path leads you, without fear. Change yourself, and that will change the world beyond all reckoning.

Trust

My child,
You are meant to write
To write the story of the journey of humanity into
Something quite different.
My child, you are meant to speak
To speak the choices we are and those we are becoming.
You are doing fine!
Do not despair
There is no wrong
There is no losing of the way
All things are as they have been agreed to be
And the detours are part of the destination.
You will see
It is all unfolding
And you cannot stop it by virtue of
A small mistake.
So breathe and trust
Keep walking the path as best you see it.
Your feet will be led
Your voice will be led
You will stand up and sing out
And the tune will be exactly right
At the right time
In the right way
And all will be as it truly is:
Magical
Universal
Doable.

Just wait, child,
And trust.
It is your ego self that frets.
Silly child!
There is no such thing as wrong!
Just messages in bottles
Taking the slow road
Home.

Ripening

Each day, as I settle
Into the clear pool of time I call meditation
(Spirit joyful
Feet flat on the floor.)
Each day I ask
What energy do I need today
In this golden moment,
In this pause along my way?
Today the answer came back
Ripening.
What a luscious word—
Ripening.
It evokes progress
My purpose that is coming clear,
The knowing that soon I shall bear fruit.

Earth, too, is ripening.
She holds the intent to grow into her next incarnation.
The fruits of her journey may be strange,
But I cannot wait
To taste them.

Doubt (1)

What do I say
To the doubters
To the ones not sure
We are more than our bodies and our minds?
What do I say
To those who doubt
The moments their own hands touched the veil and yet
They have another answer than god for it?
God.
God is the magic alive in the universe—the part
Of us that *knows*, that can
See beyond this small and mortal moment.
Well,
There is truly nothing I can say,
Except
The magic is there for all your disbelieving
And one day it might find a crack
And start to grow.

Doubt (2)

What do I say
To the doubters
To the ones not sure
Those who cannot see the phoenix
For the flame,
Who see the earthquake
But not the souls reclaimed?
If you are one for whom the godlight
Is not quite real
Then know
It fills you still
Like ruby liquor in a loving cup
Too heavy-handled
To lift up.

Breathe

Breathe.
The angels know
The light is brighter than you can receive it
Life more miraculous,
Joy sweeter—
For when we taste the pain
Puckering our lips like lemons or like salt
Our very anger claims
That we are worthy.
Breathe.
Open the wings of your heart
And know you are safe
And loved
Beyond your reckoning.

Hate Teaches

Hate teaches.
Therefore send
Gratitude and roses
To those who live hate.
Requisite pieces of the master plan,
They blossom beside us.
Without the genocide of greed, without
Death and other evil saints,
No change would flow.

Hate heals.
Therefore send
Prayers and payments to
Those whose role it is to
Plan and persecute.
Without them, truly,
It would be us
Wearing the Kalashnikovs
In honor of
The bright optimism
Of all our races.

Beneath

I sink beneath the surface of things
Where there is a realness
Solid as stones pulled wet from water
This wet stone in my hand—
Proof of earth
Question of god
Solid as a small heart beating.

I stand
I know
And I am comforted.

Meditation Stone

Great rock
From the great black heart
Of Earth
You sing me the song
Of the planet's bones
Susurrus of ancient rivers and
Evaporated roads.
Ponderous,
You weigh me down.
I sink deep into my own life
My toes tingle in the river of time
Which flows beyond this worried moment
And I flow with it
All peace
All great wide empty still
Suffused with the knowingness
Of stone.

Surrender

I surrender my ego
Into the pool of spirit

I surrender my mind
Into the hand of god

I release the stories I have long told
I yield up
My baggage and my shame

As my physical body sits
In quiet communion
So my soul
Finds god again
Finds peace again
Is light
Again
It is that simple . . .
That
Amazingly
Brilliant

Exhale

Exhale.
And with your breath
Release
All those people inside
Your head.
You love them all,
But only they
Can help themselves.
And so,
Release them.
Send love.
Know that
The highest good
Invites you to
Bless them with an outflung breath
While only you remain
Inside the center of your head.
Exhale.
Be empty.
Clear.
Even god walks not
In the dust of another's journey.

Sleep

Sit as if you rest
In the great hand of god,
Palm large enough to hold
Your ageless and physical self.
Let all your cares
Flow out and off
For how can worry stay
In the space where peace was made?
Recline.
Let anxiety waterfall away.
Know love without judgment
Guidance without demands.
See power hung like a hammock in the stars
You, the child rocked
You, the goddess napping
You, a small part of a great wheel turning
You, lustrous as the light that made you:
Sleep.

Effortless as Rain

Let my day be
Effortless as rain.
Let the magic fall
Unhindered from the spirit sky
Until it shimmers all around me.
Let me walk as light
Knowing that sustenance will come
Knowing that friends are mine
Knowing that I am in the right place at the right time
Doing the right thing,
All of which rightness opens me
To divine providence:
What I need, I will be given.
Let my day be
Effortless as rain
Joyous as a young girl
Bright as a copper kettle.
Nothing needs to be so hard—
That is an old, old truth no longer mine.
Release!
Surrender!
Splash in the puddles of now
With absolute, muddy abandon.

Joy

Spirit says:

*Ahhh, you are so bright! Can you not see yourself
shine? Will you not allow it? I, your higher self,
can see you. So light, you float
beyond imagination.*

Come Down Like Rain

Spirit come down like rain, like rain
Fill the empty places

Spirit come down like rain, like rain
Wash clear the dry and dusty spaces

Spirit come down like rain, like rain
Wash out the anger, pain, and shame

Spirit come down like rain, like rain
My body from its drought reclaim

Spirit come down like rain, like rain
And let me breathe in god again.

Joy Song

Oh, glorious day!
Here in the now of
Our human race
On a sacred journey to a new
Collective space.

This habit of peace that is mine
This cultivated connection to divine
As I sink
Into my breath and time
What a glory
To be here, to be alive!

Spring

Oh, what a joyful time this is!
A new spring on an old planet,
Old spirits in young bodies
Even the wind feels washed!

Oh, what a joyful time this is!
Woodpeckers weave the late winter woods,
Hawks dive in a sea of bliss
Many small families are feeding forth.

Oh, what a joyful time this is!
Sunlight like mead on the cool earth
Worms and buds yawn and stretch,
The future of our race unfurls before us
A future made manifest by love, and dirt.

Full Moon, New Earth

Full moon,
New earth,
And still my words pour forth.
Crown aflame
With the candles of my soul
Lifetimes have I travelled to this moment
To keep this knowledge safe:
That like a phoenix from the ash
Of her own greed,
Humanity will from turmoil rise again.

Earth cannot support
So many at one time again,
And so fewer will come back,
And more depart,
And those that remain
Have soul-sworn
To do this work—
To move forward the collective plan
To witness
And to be
The change.

Child of God

I am naked in my beauty,
Glory where I stand,
With Sun's light on my outside and
Spirit's light within.

The heavens are my playground,
I ride the starry lands.
Jubilant with laughter,
I gallop cosmic sands.

The wind outside me whispers,
It blows when I cry out.
The horses from fields are calling
I am within; they are without.

Yet I am the grass they are eating,
I am the feet that walk
I am the nose that nibbles
The rounded back, the lifted hock—

All of Source flows through me
I am it and it is mine
All of light is Spirit and
All of Spirit, mine.
I echo the song of the children—
They know I am divine.

And all of this breath is in me
And gently it flows out
In the moon and the mist and the loving
As within, so without.
As within, so without.

Utterly

Sisters,
Many lifetimes have we walked together
(Or maybe none)
And here we are come back home
Into this space
Of joyous birthing
Each one stepping like Venus
From the sea of the murky known
Onto the white glittering sand
Of the unremembered
Where each one finds her sari
Of spirit silk
Left there that long-ago lifetime
As we stepped down into the sea.

And lo! We have returned
To claim again the jeweled cloths,
Delicate beads, the fabric each had chosen,
And, wondrous,
In this lifetime we find
The dresses fit us
Utterly.

Coming Home

Call home
Call home
Oh, call me home!
Bring me into the center of time
Light like a star within me
Let me open like a lily in the dawn
Of humanity's second birthday—
A millennium older and more wise
And here we are, Beauty, come together in joy
Radiant and dancing on the bright cliff of now.

Moving Time

Water is moving
Across the planet
Stepping out of
Customary courses and
Forging new flows.

Spirit, too, is moving.
The magnetic voice of god is
Carving new channels.
Step in! Step in!
Immerse yourself
In light, join
The inexorable tsunami
Of joy.

Wave

Life is so joyful!
This time of change
Terrifies
Exhilarates
Uplifts.
We balance on the cusp of a changing planet.
As surfers greet the wave
We surrender our bodies and our hearts
Into the marriage of sun and spume
High on the curl
Seeing before us
Our own divine future.

I Am Here

I am here
I am god
I am carried by the flow

I have aspired to now
Achieving it, I find
It is as simple as
An earthworm rising through
Spring rain
Without effort, I find
The pivotal balance
Of wet and dry
Of earth and sky

I am here
And here turns out to be
Precisely my intended destination
My bones
Liquefy
With my own perfection

I See You

Oh child of god,
I see you!
You are so beautiful.
Your spirit shines out
In waves of joy
Your aura shimmers and flows
And all around you are lit like candles
From your magnificence.

Leviathan

My spirit opens
Like a rose of awe.
I breathe in wonder
Of this power I have become.
Power to see
And know
The breadth and depth of
Universe;
Power to look within,
Beyond,
And through.
Like a leviathan,
I swim the cosmic seas.
With my eyes shut,
There is a whole new world to live in.

Call to Awe

Like a leviathan,
I swim
In a sea of wonder
And awe.
All the magical empty places
Are mine to know.
When I choose,
My spirit can
Leave my body behind,
Visit the fountain
Of youth,
Be healed,
Be known,
See,
And be seen.
I can walk
In the Garden of Eden
I can peruse
The reams of history rolled
And stored
Among humanity's sacred records.
Truly, magic is afoot
In a universe
More deep, more wide, more
Wondrous
Than I ever could have
Known
Before I cleared the way

Into the secret garden of my psychic self
Before I learned to use
My own clairvoyance—
The land behind my eyes that holds
All the wisdom of the universe.
Once I lived
In the prison with five walls
And only my heart flew free.
Now all of me knows
I am god
God is me
And all of us
On Earth
Are one.
We are
Sisters to Eagles,
Brothers to Sun,
Ancient children of young love.
We must awaken
Awaken all
Awaken you.
You
Are the infinite in
A tiny drop of dew.
You
Are the ant
Rejoicing in
The beauty of
A single stem.

You
Are the child of magic
And of gods—
Awake!
For all the world is bathed in rainbows
Where you walk
And all the angels
Applaud the flame
Of more conscious being
On the road to change.

Birth

And so the veil is lifted
And so, the women dance
Dressed only in faith and promises
Feet empty of regrets

For lo! We are the glory
The wisdom, and the flame
We are heaven made manifest
We are the earth, reclaimed

And the birds know,
And the turtles know,
And the whales swim with us

We, who are the blessing
We, who are the blessed
We, both body and spirit
Together, alive, at last

See? The tsunami of Spirit
We have long sheltered in our past
This future we have carried
Is birthing us at last.

Afterword

No one else can do this for us—heal our life.

No one else can step up and sort through all the memories in our closet, culling the past and leaving only dust and space and clothing that represents the present time.

No one else can go shopping in our skin, and choose to purchase peace and leave the suffering unransomed on the grocery shelves. No one will stand over us and make our hands take time to peel and trim, chop and stir peace. No mouth but ours can chew it.

On the other hand, no soul other than ours will know the clear joy of feeling at home within our skin. Can you imagine a life without that cosmic ball and chain called expectation? Can you picture a life path clear of guilt?

In the end, how little we need in order to live. Just four walls, a roof, and the light of our incarnate self.

The Journey Continues . . .

Alix says:

I am here in this lifetime to be the change: to be part of the journey from violence to consciousness, from struggle to sufficiency, from stress to joy. I am nowhere near perfect, but I am utterly divine. You are, too.

How may I help?

Dear Reader,

These words are not my words.

These words have come through me, for me and for you and for all who are part of the transition to a new earth. And what a joyful transition it is!

I invite you to continue to travel with me as we create this new earth together. I'd love to have you drop by my website, www.yoursoulstruth.com, and check out the resources I have gathered there to help you grow your wings and live as the powerful being you truly are.

I'd love to connect. Please feel free to drop me an email at alix@yoursoulstruth.com.

In joy,

Alix

About Alix

My Spirit Says

My spirit says that I am
Here to be light, that I am
Here to be fearless,
Here to be an example.
My spirit says all is well.
My spirit says, teach peace,
Teach empowerment, teach the
Tools of living as a divine spark
Inside a human body.
Breathe.

Hi, I'm Alix.

I'm a soul healer, a soul teacher, and a powerful channel for the wisdom and healing of the Archangels. I am here to help you learn and heal so that you can fully embody your god/dess self and fulfill your mission to serve and support the evolution of planet.

Books by Alix

The Abundance Diet for Writers

The Creative Flow Toolbox: *Holistic Solutions for Writer's Block*

Full Moon, New Earth: *Poems of Joy for the Collective Journey*

The Gift: *How My Horse Taught Me to Teach the Toughest Children*

Tapping the Well Within: *Writing from Your Source of Effortless Creativity, Deep Wisdom, and Utter Joy*

Writer, the World Needs You: *Get Past Your Fear and Write the Words You're Meant to Write*

Contact Alix

Email: alix@yoursoulstruth.com

Website: www.yoursoulstruth.com

Social media
   Twitter: @YourSoulsTruth
   Facebook: YourSoulsTruth

www.ingramcontent.com/pod-product-compliance
Lightning Source LLC
Chambersburg PA
CBHW031539040426
42445CB00010B/613